RECENT RESEARCHES IN THE MUSIC OF THE BAROQUE ERA, 158

Marc-Antoine Charpentier

In nativitatem Domini canticum H. 416

Edited by Paul Walker

A-R Editions, Inc.
Middleton, Wisconsin

Performance parts are available from the publisher.

A-R Editions, Inc., Middleton, Wisconsin
© 2010 by A-R Editions, Inc.

All rights reserved. No part of this book may be reproduced or transmitted in any form by any electronic or mechanical means (including photocopying, recording, or information storage and retrieval) without permission in writing from the publisher.

The purchase of this edition does not convey the right to perform it in public, nor to make a recording of it for any purpose. Such permission must be obtained in advance from the publisher.

A-R Editions is pleased to support scholars and performers in their use of *Recent Researches* material for study or performance. Subscribers to any of the *Recent Researches* series, as well as patrons of subscribing institutions, are invited to apply for information about our "Copyright Sharing Policy."

Printed in the United States of America

ISBN-13: 978-0-89579-667-7
ISBN-10: 0-89579-667-8
ISSN: 0484-0828

♾ The paper used in this publication meets the minimum requirements of the American National Standard for Information Sciences—Permanence of Paper for Printed Library Materials, ANSI Z39.48-1992.

Contents

Acknowledgments vi

Introduction vii
   Marc-Antoine Charpentier and Sacred Music vii
   Charpentier's *In nativitatem Domini canticum,* H. 416 vii
   Performance Issues viii
   Notes ix

Text and Translation, *Translation by David Kovacs and Paul Walker* x

In nativitatem Domini canticum, H. 416
   Praeludium 1
   Chorus Justorum 3
   Nuit 23
   Réveil des Bergers 27
   Chorus Pastorum 28
   [Récit de l'Ange] 29
   [Choeur] 35
   [Pastor] 40
   Marche des Bergers 40
   [Choeur] 42
   [L'Ange seul avec Choeur] 44
   Dernier Choeur 48

Critical Report 55
   Source 55
   Editorial Methods 55
   Critical Notes 56

Acknowledgments

To begin, I would like to remember H. Wiley Hitchcock, the Dean of Charpentier studies, who died in 2007. When I first heard Les Arts Florissants's recording and wished to perform the piece, it was Wiley who appeared totally unannounced one day at my door in Charlottesville (where his daughter still lives) in order to hand me a complete manuscript score of the entire work in his own hand. (This was before the appearance of Minkoff's reprints of the Charpentier *cahiers*.) Wiley told me that he had always intended to publish his edition, made years before, but never gotten around to it, and he gave me his blessing to pursue publication myself. Now these many years later the present edition is the fulfillment of my promise to do so. It is to Wiley Hitchcock's memory that I wish to dedicate this volume.

I would also like to acknowledge the singers in my Charlottesville-based ensemble Zephyrus, whose performances of Charpentier's *In nativitatem Domini canticum*, H. 416, under my direction, have deepened both my understanding of the work and my appreciation of its beauties. One of those singers, David Kovacs, also deserves my tremendous gratitude for his work in providing the English translation of the nonbiblical portions of Charpentier's text.

Introduction

Marc-Antoine Charpentier and Sacred Music

The very first volume in the present series, Recent Researches in the Music of the Baroque Era, was devoted to a work by Marc-Antoine Charpentier,[1] as have been three subsequent volumes (48, 63, and 72), so the details of Charpentier's biography are by now well known to users of the series. The last of these biographical sketches, by David C. Rayl for volume 72, is particularly thorough,[2] and users of the present volume who wish to know more detail than provided by the thumbnail biography below are encouraged to consult it.

Charpentier's birth and death dates are now firmly established (1643–1704), as is the fact of his study in Italy with Giacomo Carissimi for an unknown period of time in the 1660s. Although the composer wrote in virtually all of the genres of late-seventeenth-century French music, easily the largest part of his output is taken up by music for the church, including eleven masses, nearly one hundred and fifty additional liturgical works of various kinds, over eighty psalm settings, and more than two hundred motets. We are exceptionally well informed about the circumstances for which Charpentier wrote the vast majority of these works. In 1670 he entered the service of Mademoiselle de Guise, the last surviving member of the house of Lorraine, which maintained the family residence in Paris. It appears that family connections between the Charpentier and Guise families got the composer this first important position, and he seems to have served Mlle de Guise until sometime in the mid 1680s, when he was named *maître de musique* for the church of Saint-Louis, the principal church of the Jesuits in Paris. There is no record of his resignation from this position, but in 1698 Charpentier was chosen *maître de musique* at the Sainte-Chapelle, which position he held until his death.

Each of these three posts offered more prestige and grander resources than the one before. The household of Mlle de Guise is described in great detail in an article by Patricia Ranum.[3] Its patron was very devout, and life in her court included daily Mass, special Masses and Vespers on feast days, and a great many concerts that were, according to Ranum, "predominantly spiritual."[4] When Charpentier moved to the Jesuit church of Saint-Louis he took a post that, according to Sébastien de Brossard, ranked "among the most brilliant" in all of France,[5] with well-known singers from the opéra frequently to be heard there. Finally, the Sainte-Chapelle boasted some of the finest church music in all of France, and Charpentier wrote some of his most opulent pieces for it. It was almost certainly for the second of these places, the church of Saint-Louis, that Charpentier wrote his Christmas piece *In nativitatem Domini canticum*, H. 416, which is thought to date from the late 1680s.

Charpentier's *In nativitatem Domini canticum*, H. 416

Almost none of Charpentier's sacred music was published during his lifetime, but we are extremely fortunate that the composer meticulously copied out most of it himself in fair copy in a series of notebooks now to be found in the Bibliothèque nationale de France in Paris. Charpentier's copy of H. 416 is the only known exemplar of the piece, and it is remarkably free from errors.[6] The Latin text, by an unknown librettist, falls into two halves. The first takes on an Advent or Old Testament nature and is derived from Psalm 12:1 in the Vulgate (13:1 in the English Bible): "Usquequo, Domine, obliviscateris me in finem? Usquequo avertis faciem tuam a me?" (How long wilt thou forget me, O Lord? forever? How long wilt thou hide thy face from me?) The second half tells in more theatrical manner the familiar story of the angels and the shepherds as related in Luke 2:8–20. To separate the two halves Charpentier provided a beautiful little instrumental tone poem depicting night as the shepherds watch over their sheep, which movement the composer called simply "Nuit." This brief tone poem has proven to be quite popular in modern times: the Charpentier thematic catalog lists four recordings of it (without the rest of the piece) that appeared between 1951 and 1977, the earliest in 78 rpm format.[7] The piece in its entirety was first recorded by William Christie and Les Arts Florissants in 1983,[8] but no modern edition of the whole has appeared before the present one.

Scholars do not entirely agree on the proper genre designation for this and other similar works by Charpentier. Because of his study with Carissimi, the father of the baroque oratorio, Charpentier's sacred works based on biblical and other religious stories are generally thought of and referred to as oratorios. In the entry for Charpentier in *New Grove*, however, H. Wiley Hitchcock argues instead for the designation "dramatic motet" in the tradition of the French *grand motet*, in large part because of the intended use of such pieces within liturgical services rather than in the extra-liturgical contexts in which Carissimi's oratorios were heard.[9] Whatever the various pieces' relationship to official liturgy, the differences in musical style between dramatic motet and oratorio are negligible. Both feature solo and chorus with orchestral accompaniment, and both tell stories using individual characters who sing solo recitatives and airs and collective groups who may alternately participate in the action and comment on it. Our piece, for instance, includes parts for, in its first half, the "Chorus Justorum" (Chorus of the Just) and, in its second half, "L'Ange" (the Angel), the host of angels (not explicitly labeled in the score but identified in the text), and the shepherds ("Pastors"), both individual and collective. Charpentier also provides descriptive instrumental movements that set the mood and further the story, including, in addition to "Nuit," the "Réveil des Bergers" (Awakening of the Shepherds [by the Angels]) and the "Marche des Bergers" as the shepherds travel to Bethlehem. The entire work lasts about half an hour in performance and would fit well into a Christmas Day service that took as its principal text the passage from Luke 2.

Performance Issues

In nativitatem, H. 416, is set for four-part vocal and four-part instrumental ensemble. Particular instruments are not specified at the beginning of Charpentier's autograph copy, but indications later in the piece make clear that we are to understand strings in four parts, "flûtes" (still in the late seventeenth century referring to recorders rather than transverse flutes), and organ. Charpentier asks that the instrumental bass line be provided with a sub-group to accompany most of the solo singing (indicated in the score with "acc[ompagnement] seul"). This sub-group should comprise, according to a note at measure 516, more than one string instrument ("vio[lo]ns") and organ, which suggests for the whole work an instrumental ensemble of some considerable size, befitting a church of the prestige and reputation of Saint-Louis. Charpentier's orchestration is carefully worked out and clearly indicated: the recorders come and go from the texture (they are absent from "Nuit," for example, but prominent in the following "Réveil des Bergers"), and the composer even requests mutes for the string instruments in "Nuit." The four instrumental clefs are French violin, soprano, mezzo-soprano, and bass, a cleffing that places the second part relatively low for violin or rather high for viola and the third part relatively high for viola. In Charpentier's day the two inner parts in soprano and mezzo-soprano clef were probably played on violas of two different sizes rather than on violins.

Three sections—measures 106–86, the solo portions of measures 652–83, and those of measures 692–730—have a reduced texture of two high instruments, one solo voice, and basso continuo; in these instances, the two instrumental parts both carry French violin clef. At the conclusion of the first of these sections, measure 186 (the beginning of a new system), the first note of the top part in the score is stemmed both up and down, indicating that both obbligato parts in the preceding section are taken from the top part, which is in French violin clef throughout. For the portions of the latter two sections involving chorus the second part from the top reverts to soprano clef. It seems most likely, then, that Charpentier intended for the recorders to play together on the top line throughout the piece and divide only when two parts in French violin clef are given, that is, when the top violin section divides. Furthermore, in measure 700 the two parts are notated together on the top staff with up and down stemming, although in measures 692–96 they are notated on the top two staves. Charpentier's indications for the instrumentation for these sections introduce a small inconsistency. At measure 106, where both the top violin and flûte divide, the upper part is given in the plural ("vio[lo]ns et fl") but the lower in the singular ("vio[lo]n et fl"). At measure 652, with recorders only, we find the plural ("fl seules") in both parts. Charpentier's isolated use of the singular at measure 106 seems likely, then, to be a simple copying error, and he almost certainly intended for the entire top violin section, along with all of the recorders, to divide into two equal halves for these moments of reduced texture. It is an indication of the impressive size of Charpentier's instrumental resources at Saint-Louis that he could think in terms of at least four recorders for such a performance.

The four vocal parts carry treble, alto, tenor, and bass clefs. There are no solos for soprano; the most extended of the solo parts is that of the Angel in measures 408–521, notated in alto clef, and there are also shorter solo parts at various points for both tenor and bass. Indications of "seul" and "tous" for the alto part in measures 652–83 and those for "P[remiè]re Basse" (m. 692) and "S[econ]de Basse seul[e]" (m. 700) make clear that Charpentier envisioned at least two singers per vocal part. Given the prestige enjoyed by the church of Saint-Louis, a sizable chorus might well have been the norm, especially for such an important feast day as Christmas. The soprano parts of Charpentier's sacred music were variously sung by boys and by women, depending on circumstances. Women certainly sang sacred music in the household of Mlle de Guise, but in most of the important churches boy sopranos were the rule. The prominence of opera singers at Saint-Louis, however, makes the possibility of women sopranos more likely there, although they might have been employed primarily in solo rather than than in choral contexts. Nevertheless, there was clearly no ban on women singing before the congregation at Saint-Louis. Charpentier's score for *In nativitatem* offers no helpful clues regarding the voices: we find neither indications of voice types nor the names of any individual singers.

As is by now well known, the pitch of French organs was low, around A = 392, approximately a whole step below our modern pitch, and *In nativitatem* was almost certainly conceived for and performed at this standard pitch for French sacred music.[10] Rare indeed is the ensemble today that can produce both an organ and recorders capable of playing at that pitch, not to mention string players willing to tune their instruments down so far from modern A. Even Les Arts Florissants in 1983 chose to record the piece at A = 415, the usual standard for modern baroque orchestras. Perhaps the greatest difference produced by the low pitch is to be seen in the voice parts: the Angel's solo, for instance, is transformed from a part with a high note of a' (reached many times) to one of g' at modern pitch, that is, from a part comfortably within the alto range to one readily singable by a light tenor with a secure and relaxed high G. *In nativitatem* clearly "works" at any one of these three pitches, although the lower its pitch the warmer and richer its sound is likely to be.

Two performance conventions of French baroque music also deserve mention: *notes inégales* and the profuse ornamentation beloved by the French. Charpentier uses the squiggle to indicate a trill, and he sprinkles them liberally throughout his score. These should be done beginning on the upper, dissonant note. Opportunities for the application of *notes inégales* are less to be found in the first, somber part than in the joyous second part with its lively solos and dance-based March to Bethlehem. Naturally, the inequality would be applied to pairs of eighth notes.

Notes

1. Marc-Antoine Charpentier, *Judicium Salomonis*, ed. H. Wiley Hitchcock, Recent Researches in the Music of the Baroque Era, vol. 1 (New Haven, Conn.: A-R Editions, 1964).

2. Idem, *Nine Settings of the "Litanies de la Vierge,"* ed. David C. Rayl, Recent Researches in the Music of the Baroque Era, vol. 72 (Madison, Wis.: A-R Editions, 1994), vii–viii. The other two volumes are *Vocal Chamber Music*, ed. John S. Powell, vol. 48 (1986), and *Music for Molière's Comedies*, ed. John S. Powell, vol. 63 (1990).

3. "A Sweet Servitude: A Musician's Life at the Court of Mlle de Guise," *Early Music* 15 (1987): 347–60.

4. Ibid., 354.

5. See *The New Grove Dictionary of Music and Musicians*, 2nd ed. (hereafter *NG2*), s.v. "Charpentier, Marc-Antoine" (p. 506), by H. Wiley Hitchcock.

6. See the published facsimile edition, Marc-Antoine Charpentier, *Oeuvres complètes I: Meslanges autographes*, vol. 9 (Paris: Minkoff, 1997), fols. 51v–61r.

7. H. W. Hitchcock, *Les Oevres de Marc-Antoine Charpentier: Catalogue raisonné* (Paris: Picard, 1982), 309–10.

8. M. A. Charpentier, *Un Oratorio de Noël*, Les Arts Florissants, dir. William Christie (Harmonia Mundi France, HMC 905130, 1983).

9. *NG2*, "Charpentier," 507–8.

10. For the details concerning French pitch at this time, see Bruce Haynes, *A History of Performing Pitch: The Story of "A"* (Lanham, Md.: The Scarecrow Press, 2002), 97–102.

Text and Translation

Translation by David Kovacs and Paul Walker

Praeludium

TAILLE

Usquequo avertis faciem tuam, Domine, et oblivisceris tribulationis nostrae?

Comment. Adapted from Psalm 12:1.

Chorus Justorum

CHOEUR

Memorare testamenti tui quod locutus es; veni, veni de excelso et libera nos.

PREMIÈRE BASSE

Consolare, filia Sion; quare maerore consumeris? Consolare, filia Sion; veniet ecce Rex tibi mansuetus; plorans nequaquam plorabis, et tacebit pupilla oculi tui. In illa die stillabunt montes dulcedinem, et colles fluent lac et mel. Consolare, filia Sion; et sustine Deum, salvatorem tuum.

CHOEUR

Utinam dirumperes coelos, redemptor noster, et descenderes!

Comment. From Isaiah 64:1.

SECONDE BASSE

Prope est ut veniat Dominus; veniet et non mentietur; juxta est salus Domini qui venturus est; modo veniet qui mittendus est; veniet et non tardabit.

CHOEUR

Rorate, coeli, desuper, et nubes pluant justum; aperiatur terra et germinet salvatorem.

Comment. Introit, Advent IV.

Nuit

Réveil des Bergers

Prelude

TENOR

How long will you turn away your face, Lord, and forget our tribulation?

Chorus of the Just

CHORUS

Be mindful of your witness which you have spoken; come, come from on high and free us.

FIRST BASS

Be comforted, daughter of Sion; why are you consumed with grief? Be comforted, daughter of Sion; behold, the King will come to you in meekness; weeping, you will weep in vain, and the pupil of your eye will be silent. On that day the mountains will drip with sweetness, and the hills will flow with milk and honey. Be comforted, daughter of Sion, and support the Lord your savior.

CHORUS

Would that you would rend the heavens, our Redeemer, and come down!

SECOND BASS

The Lord's coming is nigh; he will come and will not be false; nigh is the salvation of the Lord who is to come; now he will come who was to be sent; he will come now; he will come and not delay.

CHORUS

Let dew fall, heavens, from above, and let the clouds pour forth their proper rain; let the earth be opened and bring forth the savior as a shoot.

Night

Awakening of the Shepherds

Chorus Pastorum	*Chorus of the Shepherds*

Coeli aperti sunt! lux magna orta est! lux magna, lux terribilis!

The heavens have opened! A great light has arisen! A great light, a terrible light!

[Récit de l'Ange]

The Angel's Solo

Nolite timere, pastores, ecce enim annuntio vobis gaudium magnum quod erit omni populo; quia natus est vobis hodie salvator Christus Dominus in civitate David. Et hoc erit vobis signum: invenietis infantem pannis involutum et positum in praesepio. Surgite ergo, ite, properate et adorate Dominum. Vos autem, angeli, cantate mecum Domino canticum novum quia mirabilia fecit super terram.

Do not be afraid, shepherds, for behold, I announce to you a great joy which shall be to all people; for there has been born to you today a savior, Christ the Lord, in the city of David. And this shall be a sign to you: you will find an infant wrapped in swaddling clothes and lying in a manger. Arise, therefore; go, hasten, and adore the Lord. You angels, sing with me a new song to the Lord, for he has done wondrous things on earth.

    Comment.   From Luke 2:10–13.

[Choeur]

Chorus

Gloria in altissimis Deo, et in terra pax hominibus bonae voluntatis.

Glory to God in the highest and on earth peace to men of good will.

    Comment.   Luke 2:14.

[Pastor]

A Shepherd

Transeamus usque Bethlehem et videamus hoc verbum quod factum est, quod Dominus ostendit nobis.

Let us go to Bethlehem and see this thing that has come to pass, which the Lord has shown to us.

    Comment.   From Luke 2:15.

Marche des Bergers

March of the Shepherds

[Choeur]

Chorus

O infans, o Deus, o salvator noster, sic eges, sic clamas, sic friges, sic amas, o salvator noster.

O babe, O God, O our savior, so needy you are, so loud is your cry, so cold you are, so great is your love, O our savior!

[L'Ange seul avec Choeur]

Angel alone with Chorus

[1.] Pastores undique certent concentibus; pastorum hodie natus est Dominus. Certent muneribus, certent amoribus; palmas victori legite.
[2.] Agni cum matribus caulis prorumpite; aquae de fontibus agros perfundite. Aves in vallibus concordent cantibus; silvae lac et mel facite.

1. Let shepherds everywhere vie in harmony; today is born the Lord of the shepherds. Let them vie with gifts, let them vie in love; gather palms for the victor.
2. Lambs, burst forth from the fold with your mothers; waters of the fountains, pour forth over the fields. Let the birds in the valleys sing in harmony; forests, make milk and honey.

Dernier Choeur

Final Chorus

Exultemus, jubilemus Deo salutari nostro. Justitia regnabit in terra nostra, et pacis non erit finis.

Let us exult, let us rejoice in the Lord our salvation. Justice will reign in the land, and of peace there will be no end.

    Comment.   From Isaiah 9:7.

In nativitatem Domini canticum, H. 416

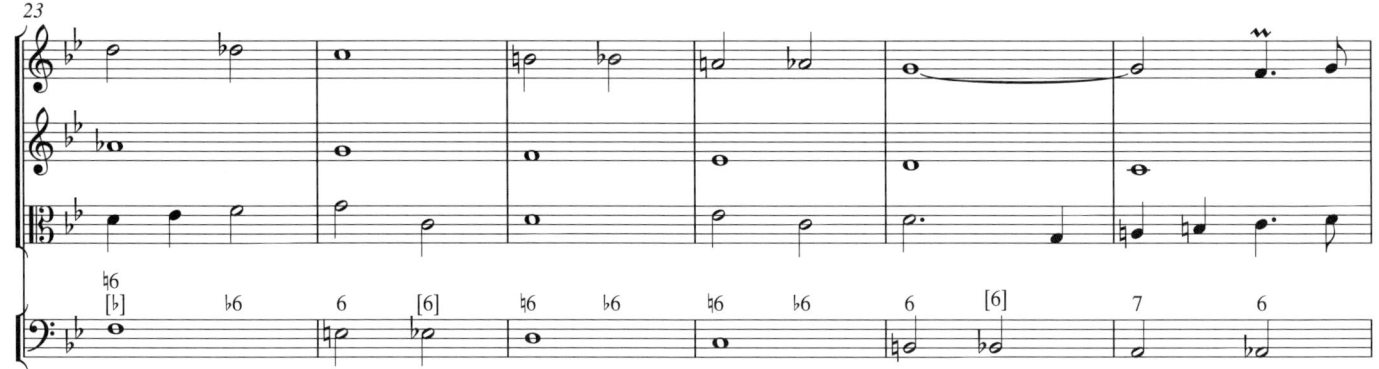

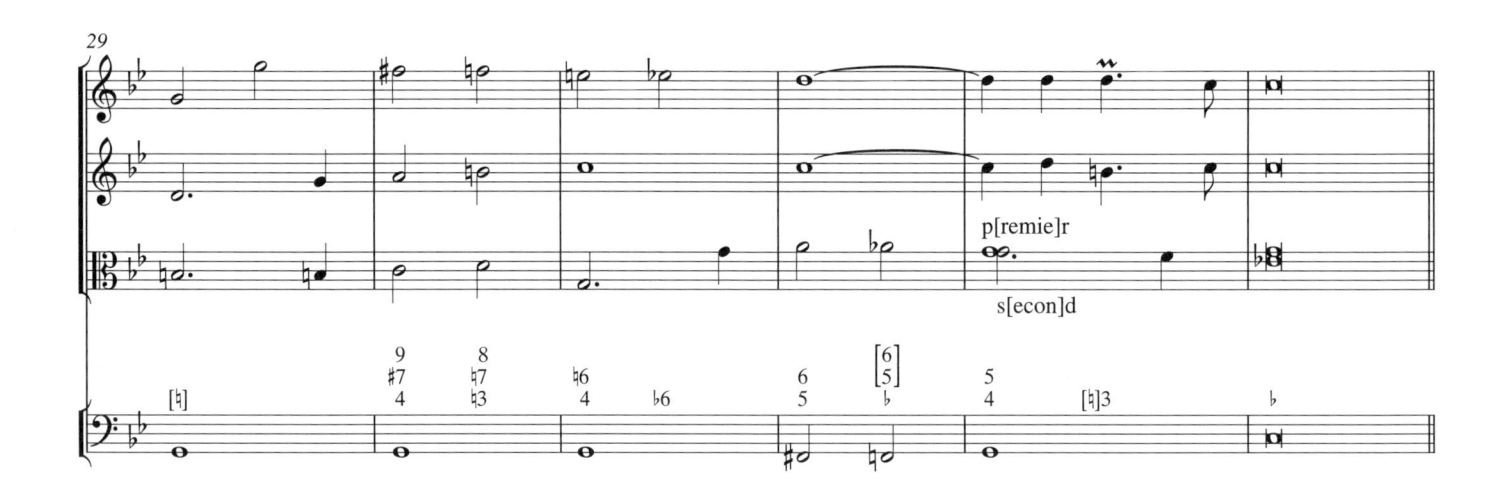

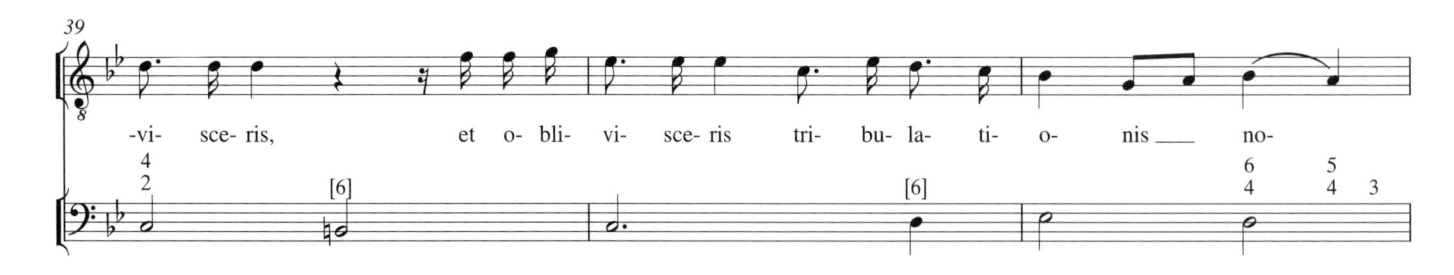

Us- que- quo, us- que quo a- ver- tis fa- ci- em tu- am, Do- mi- ne, et o-bli- -vi- sce- ris, et o- bli- vi- sce- ris tri- bu- la- ti- o- nis no-

[accompagnement seul]

-strae? Us- que- quo, us- que- quo a- ver- tis fa- ci- em tu- am, Do- mi- ne, et o- bli- vi- sce- ris, et o- bli- vi- sce- ris tri- bu- la- ti- -o- nis, tri- bu- la- ti- o- nis no- strae?

Chorus Justorum
tous vio[lo]ns et fl[ûtes]

Me- mo- ra- re, me- mo- ra- re, me- mo- ra- re, me- mo- ra- re te- sta- men- ti tu- i
Me- mo- ra- re, me- mo- ra- re, me- mo- ra- re, me- mo- ra- re te- sta- men- ti tu- i
Me- mo- ra- re, me- mo- ra- re, me- mo- ra- re, me- mo- ra- re te- sta- men- ti tu- i
Me- mo- ra- re, me- mo- ra- re, me- mo- ra- re te- sta- men- ti tu- i

tous vio[lo]ns et basse cont[inue]   acc. seul   tous

55
quod lo- cu- tus es; me- mo- ra- re, me- mo-ra- re, me- mo-
quod lo- cu- tus es; me- mo- ra- re, me- mo-ra- re, me- mo-
quod lo- cu- tus es; me- mo- ra- re, me- mo-ra- re, me- mo-
quod lo- cu- tus es; me- mo-ra- re, me- mo-
59
-ra- re te- sta-men-ti tu- i quod lo- cu- tus es;
-ra- re te- sta-men-ti tu- i quod lo- cu- tus es;
-ra- re te- sta- men-ti tu- i quod lo- cu- tus es;
-ra- re te- sta-men-ti tu- i quod lo- cu- tus es;

63
ve- ni, ve- ni, ve- ni, ve- ni, ve- ni, ve- ni de ex-
ve- ni, ve- ni, ve- ni, ve- ni, ve- ni, ve- ni de ex-
ve- ni, ve- ni, ve- ni, ve- ni, ve- ni, ve- ni de ex-
ve- ni, ve- ni, ve- ni, ve- ni, ve- ni, ve- ni de ex-
69
-cel- - so, de ex- cel- so et li- be- ra nos, et
-cel- - so, de ex- cel- so et li- be- ra nos, et
-cel- so, de ex- cel- so et li- be- ra nos, et
-cel- so, ve- ni de ex- cel- so et

li- be- ra, et li- be- ra nos;
li- be- ra, et li- be- ra nos;
li- be- ra, li- be- ra nos;
li- be- ra, et li- be- ra nos;

ve- ni, ve- ni, ve- ni,
ve- ni, ve- ni, ve- ni,
ve- ni, ve- ni, ve- ni,
ve- ni, ve- ni, ve- ni,

87
ve- ni, ve- ni, ve- ni de ex- cel- so, de ex- cel- so et
ve- ni, ve- ni, ve- ni de ex- cel- so, de ex- cel- so et
ve- ni, ve- ni, ve- ni de ex- cel- so, de ex- cel- so et
ve- ni, ve- ni, ve- ni de ex- cel- so, de ex- cel- so et
93
li- be- ra nos; ve- ni, ve- ni de ex- cel- so, de ex-
li- be- ra nos; ve- ni, ve- ni de ex- cel- so
li- be- ra nos; ve- ni, ve- - ni de ex-
li- be- ra nos; ve- ni, ve- ni de ex- cel- so

99
-cel- so et li- be- ra nos, et li- be- ra nos.
et li- be- ra nos, et li- - be- ra nos.
-cel- so et li- be- ra nos, et li- be- ra, li- - be- ra nos.
et li- be- ra nos, et li- - be- ra nos.
106
[D.vn. 1] [Fl. 1]
vio[lo]ns et fl[ûtes]
[D.vn. 2] [Fl. 2]
vio[lo]n[s] et fl[ûtes]
P[remiè]re Basse
[B1]
Con- so- la- re, con- so- la- re, fi- li- a Si- on;
[B.c.]
acc. seul
112
qua- re mae- ro- - re con- su- me-

118
-ris? Con- so- la- re,
124
con- so- la- re, fi- li- a Si- on; ve- ni- et ec- ce Rex
130
ti- bi man- su- e- - tus; plo- - rans ne-
136
-qua- quam plo- ra- bis, et ta- ce- bit,

et ta-ce-bit pu-pil-la o-cu-li tu- i.

In il-la di- e stil-la- -bunt mon-tes dul-ce-di-nem,

et col-les, et col-les flu-ent lac et mel, flu-

11

186
tous
[D.vn. 1, 2]
[Fl. 1, 2]
[Hc.vn.]
[T.vn.]
[tous]
[D]
U- ti-nam, u- ti- nam di- rum- pe-res coe- los, di- rum- pe-res
tous
[HC]
U- ti-nam, u- ti- nam di- rum- pe-res coe- los, di- rum- pe-res coe- los, di-
tous
[T]
U- ti-nam, u- ti- nam di- rum- pe-res coe- los, di- rum- pe-res
tous
[B]
-um. U- ti-nam di- rum- pe-res coe- los, di- rum- pe-res coe- los, di-
[B.c.]
[6]
tous
189
coe- los, re- dem-ptor no- ster, et de- scen- de- res, re- dem-ptor
-rum- pe-res coe- los, re- dem-ptor no- ster, et de- scen- de- res, re- dem-ptor
coe- los, re- dem-ptor no- ster, et de- scen- de- res, et de- scen- de-
-rum- pe-res coe- los, re- dem-ptor no- ster, et de- scen- de- res, et de-
[6] 9 5 6 [6] 7 6 [6] [6]

no- ster, et de- scen- de- res!

no- ster, et de- scen- de- res, et de- scen- de- res!

-res, et de- scen- de- res, et de- scen- de- res!

-scen- de- res, et de- scen- de- res!

198
[D.vn. 1, 2]
[Fl. 1, 2]
[Hc.vn.]
[T.vn.]
[B2]
[B.c.]
tous
S[econ]de Basse
Pro- pe est, pro- pe est ut ve- ni- at Do- mi- nus;
acc. seul
tous
201
ve- ni- et et non men- ti- e- tur,
ve- ni- et et non men- ti-
acc. seul
tous
acc. seul
204
-e- tur; ju- xta est, ju- xta est sa- lus Do- mi- ni
tous

qui ven- tu- rus est; mo- do ve- ni- et
acc. seul tous

qui mit- ten- dus est; ve- ni- et mo- do ve- ni- et, ve- ni- et et non tar- da-
acc. seul tous acc. seul

-bit; non, non tar- da- bit; mo- do ve- ni- et,
tous acc. seul tous acc. seul tous

16

ve- ni-et, ve- ni-et mo-do, ve- ni-et et non tar- da- bit.

acc. seul   tous

Ro- ra- te, ro- ra- te, coe- li, de- su- per, ro-

Ro- ra- te, coe- li, de- su- per, ro-

Ro- ra-

acc. seul   tous

17

232
nu- bes plu- ant, et nu- bes plu- ant ju- stum, et nu- bes
-bes plu- - ant, et nu- bes, nu- bes plu- ant, nu-
nu- bes, et nu- bes, et nu- bes, et nu-
-ant ju- stum, et nu- bes plu- ant, plu- ant

237
plu- ant ju- - stum;
- bes plu- ant ju- stum;
-bes plu- ant ju- stum;
ju- - stum;

19

20

-to- rem;
-to- rem;
-to- rem;
-to- rem;

a- pe- ri- a- tur ter- ra, a- pe- ri- a- tur ter- ra
a- pe- ri- a- tur ter- ra, a- pe- ri- a- tur ter- ra
a- pe- ri- a- tur ter- ra, a- pe- ri- a- tur ter- ra
a- pe- ri- a- tur ter- ra   et

acc. seul   tous

21

Passez ala Suite apres un peu de Silence

Nuit
Tous lentement
sans fl[ûtes]

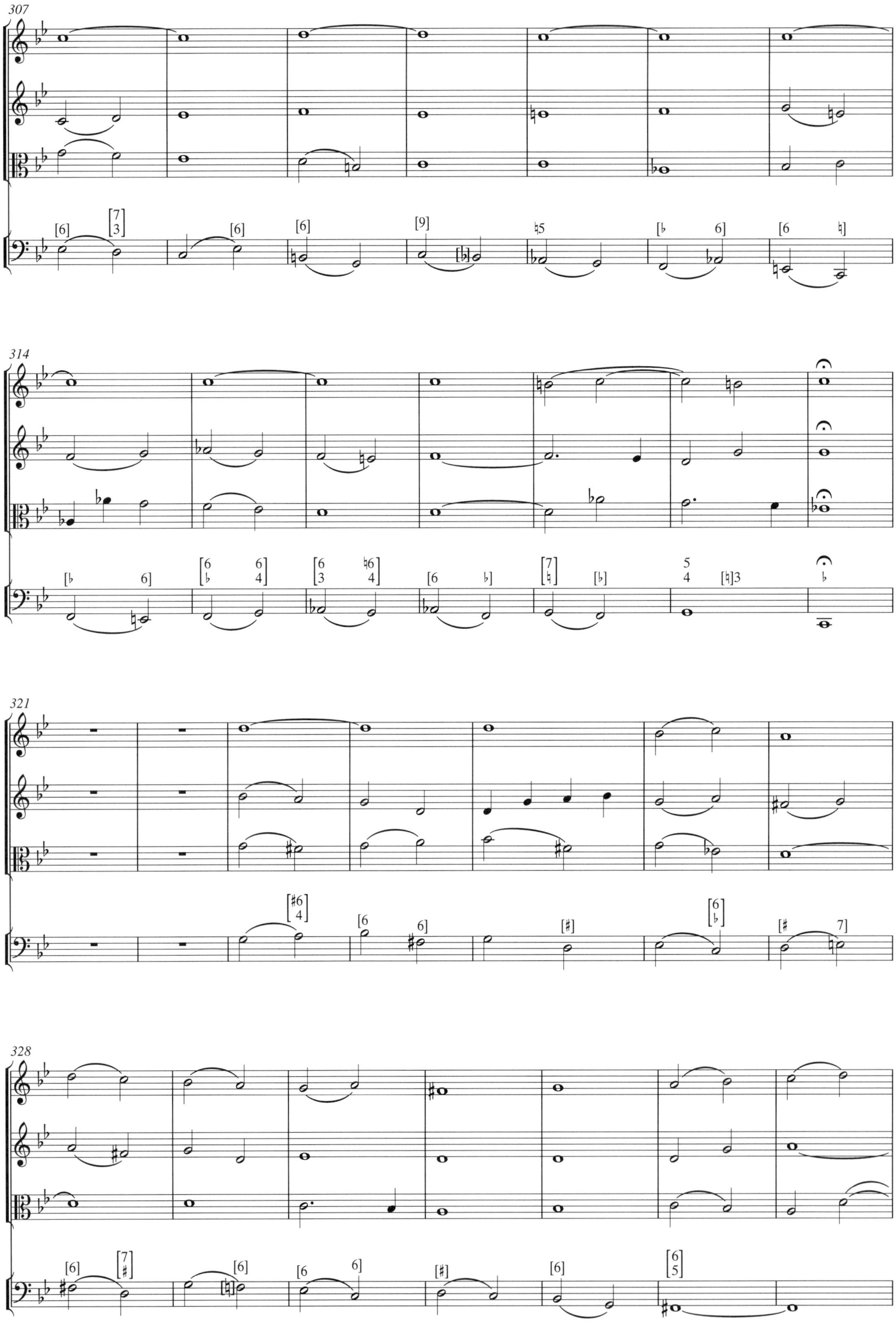
307
314
321
328

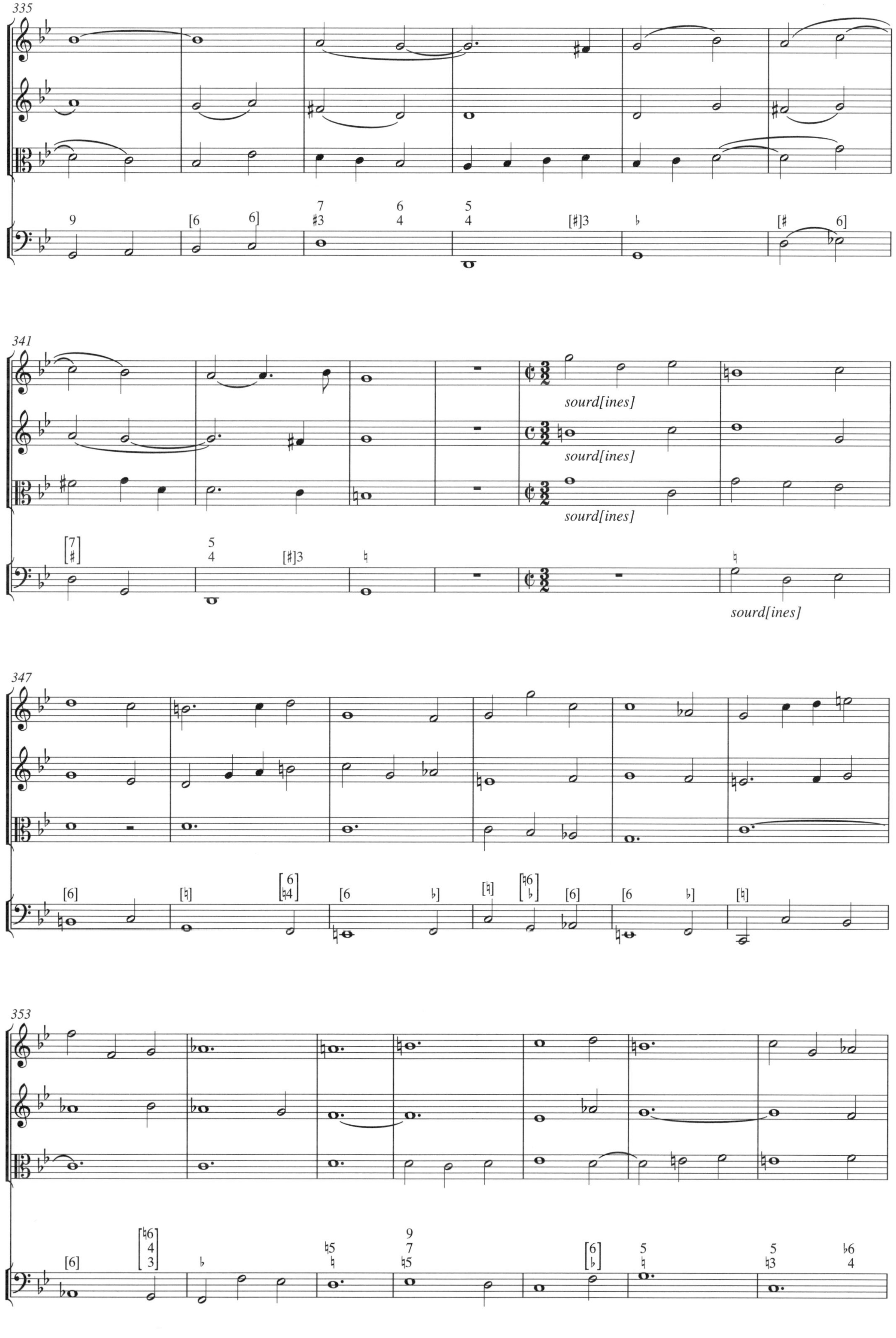
335
341
sourd[ines]
sourd[ines]
sourd[ines]
sourd[ines]
347
353

Suivez apres les deux pauses au réveil des Bergers

Réveil des Bergers

Suivez au recit del Ange apres la mesure de Silence

29

30

quia natus est vobis hodie

acc. seul

salvator Christus Dominus in civitate David.

tous

Et hoc

[acc. seul]

470
e- rit vo- bis si- gnum: in- ve- ni- e- tis in-fan- tem
tous
acc. seul
477
pan- nis in- vo- lu- tum et po- si- tum in prae- se- pi- o.
tous
483
p[remie]r
s[econ]d
Sur- - - gi- te,
acc. seul

sur- gi- te er- go, i- te, i- te, pro-pe- ra- te, tous

i- te, i- te, pro- pe- ra- te et ad- o- ra- te, et ad- o-
acc. seul

-ra- te Do- mi- num, et ad- o- ra- te, et ad- o- ra- te

508
Do- mi- num.
tous
514
Vos au- tem, an- ge- li, can- ta- te, can- ta- te me- cum
acc. seul
voix vio[lo]ns et orgue
518
Do- mi-no can- ti-cum no- vum qui- a mi- ra- bi- li- a fe- cit su- per ter- ram.

35

-tis- si- mis, in al- tis- si- mis De- o,

-tis- si- mis, in al- tis- si- mis De- o,

-tis- si- mis, in al- tis- si- mis De- o,

-tis- si- mis, in al- tis- si- mis De- o,

37

554
et in ter- ra
pax,
et in
[6]
7 6 5
♯3 4 4 [♯]3
561
pax ho- mi- ni- bus, ho- mi- ni- bus bo- nae vo- lun- ta- tis, bo-
pax, et in ter- ra pax ho-
ter- ra pax ho- mi- ni- bus bo- nae vo- lun- ta-
pax, et in ter- ra pax ho- mi- ni-
[7] [6] [6] 7 [♯]6

566
- - nae vo- - lun- ta- tis.
-mi- ni- bus bo- - nae vo- lun- ta- tis.
-tis, bo- nae vo- lun- ta- - tis.
-bus bo- nae vo- lun- ta- - tis.
571
[6]

Suivez ala marche des bergers sans interruption

Marche des Bergers

Faites apres la reprise de cette marche une petite Pause

[Choeur]
Lent
612
[D.vn. 1, 2]
[Fl. 1, 2]
[Hc.vn.]
[T.vn.]
[D]
O in- fans, o De- us, o sal- va- tor no-
[HC]
O in- fans, o De- us, o sal- va- tor no-
[T]
O in- fans, o De- us, o sal- va- tor no-
[B]
O in- fans, o De- us, o sal- va- tor no-
[B.c.]
tous
619
-ster, o sal- va- tor no- - ster, sic
-ster, o sal- va- tor no- - ster, sic
-ster, o sal- va- - tor no- ster, sic
-ster, o sal- va- tor no- - ster, sic
acc. seul

43

[L'Ange seul avec Choeur]

o salvator, salvator noster.
o salvator noster.
o salvator noster.
o salvator noster.

acc. seul tous

fl[ûtes] seules
fl[ûtes] seules
celuy qui a fait l'Ange seul

[1.] Pa- sto- res un- di- que cer- tent con- cen- ti- bus;
[2.] A- gni cum ma- tri- bus cau- lis pro- rum- pi- te;

acc. seul
l'orgue joue [avec] les fl[ûtes]

pa- sto- rum ho- di- e na- tus est Do- mi- nus.
a- quae de fon- ti- bus a- gros per- fun- di- te.

660 tous avec vio[lo]ns
[D.vn. 1, 2]
[Fl. 1, 2]
[tous avec violons]
[Hc.vn.]
[tous]
[T.vn.]
tous
[D]
Pa- sto- res un- di- que cer- tent con- cen- ti- bus;
A- gni cum ma- tri- bus cau- lis pro- rum- pi- te;
tous
[HC]
Pa- sto- res un- di- que cer- tent con- cen- ti- bus;
A- gni cum ma- tri- bus cau- lis pro- rum- pi- te;
tous
[T]
Pa- sto- res un- di- que cer- tent con- cen- ti- bus;
A- gni cum ma- tri- bus cau- lis pro- rum- pi- te;
tous
[B]
Pa- sto- res un- di- que cer- tent con- cen- ti- bus;
A- gni cum ma- tri- bus cau- lis pro- rum- pi- te;
[B.c.]
tous
664
pa- sto- rum ho- di- e na- tus est Do- mi- nus.
a- quae de fon- ti- bus a- gros per- fun- di- te.

668
fl[ûtes] seules
[Fl. 1]
[flûtes seules]
[Fl. 2]
seul
[HC]
Cer- tent mu- ne- ri- bus, cer- tent a- mo- ri- bus;
A- ves in val- li- bus con- cor- dent can- ti- bus;
[6] [6]
[B.c.]
acc. seul
672
pal- mas vi- cto- ri le- gi- te.
sil- vae lac et mel fa- ci- te.
[♯] 6 5 ♯3 ♮
676
tous avec vio[lo]ns
[D.vn. 1, 2]
[Fl. 1, 2]
[tous avec violons]
[Hc.vn.]
[T.vn.]
[D]
Cer- tent mu- ne- ri- bus, cer- tent a- mo- ri- bus;
A- ves in val- li- bus con- cor- dent can- ti- bus;
tous
[HC]
Cer- tent mu- ne- ri- bus, cer- tent a- mo- ri- bus;
A- ves in val- li- bus con- cor- dent can- ti- bus;
[T]
Cer- tent mu- ne- ri- bus, cer- tent a- mo- ri- bus;
A- ves in val- li- bus con- cor- dent can- ti- bus;
[B]
Cer- tent mu- ne- ri- bus, cer- tent a- mo- ri- bus;
A- ves in val- li- bus con- cor- dent can- ti- bus;
[6] ♯6
[B.c.]
tous

Racommencez cette chanson sur les secondes paroles et la finissez par ta ritornello puis passer ala Suite

48

Dernier Choeur

700
vio[lo]ns et fl[ûtes]
-stro.
-stro.
-stro.
S[econ]de Basse seul[e]
-stro. Ju- sti- ti- a re- gna- bit, ju- sti- ti- a re- gna- bit in
acc. seul
705
ter- ra no- stra, ju- sti- ti- a re- gna- bit in ter- ra no-

711
seul
Ex- ul- te- mus, ju- bi- le- mus De- o sa- lu- ta- ri no-
-stra,
715
tous
Ex- ul- te- mus, ju- bi- le- mus De- o sa- lu- ta- ri no-
Ex- ul- te- mus, ju- bi- le- mus De- o sa- lu- ta- ri no-
tous
-stro, ex- ul- te- mus, ju- bi- le- mus De- o sa- lu- ta- ri no-
tous
ex- ul- te- mus, ju- bi- le- mus De- o sa- lu- ta- ri no-
tous

-stro. Ju- sti- ti- a re- gna- bit, ju- sti- ti- a re- gna- bit in ter- ra no-stra, ju- sti- ti- a re- gna- bit in ter- ra, in ter- ra no- stra,

731 Plus lent
et pa- - cis non e- - rit
et pa- - cis non e- rit fi- nis, non e- rit
et pa- - cis non e- rit, non e- rit fi-
et pa- cis non e- rit fi-
737
fi- nis, et pa- cis non e- rit, non e-
fi- nis, et pa- - cis non e- rit fi-
- nis, et pa- - cis non e- rit, non
- nis, et pa- cis non e- rit

744
p[remie]r
s[econ]d
- rit fi- nis, et pa- cis non e- rit fi- nis, et pa-
-nis, non e- rit fi- nis, non e- rit fi- nis, et pa- cis, et
e- rit fi- - nis, et pa- cis non e- rit fi- - nis, et
fi- - nis, non e- rit fi- nis, et pa-
7 6
♯3 4 4 [♯]3 ♯ [7] [6]

750
- cis non e- rit fi- nis, non e- rit fi- - nis.
pa- cis non e- - rit fi- nis.
pa- cis non e- rit fi- nis, non e- rit fi- nis.
-cis non e- rit, non e- rit fi- - nis.
9 8 7 6 5
7 6 7 6 3 4 4 3

Critical Report

Source

Paris, Bibliothèque nationale, Rés. Vm[1] 259, fols. 51v–61r. A facsimile edition is available: Marc-Antoine Charpentier, *Oeuvres complètes I: Meslanges autographes*, vol. 9 (Paris: Minkoff, 1997).

Editorial Methods

Not only is Charpentier's autograph hand relatively error-free, but it is also clear and easy to read. In fact, were it not for the many and varied clefs, a modern musician could read from it with little difficulty, especially given its regular and uncomplicated barring. A few differences from standard modern notation are to be found, however, as noted in the following discussion of editorial policies.

The original note values and meter signatures of the source have been maintained. In triple meter (e.g., m. 106ff.), the value of a quarter note is represented by Charpentier as a half note with a single flag; these are set as quarter notes in the edition. The measures of the work are continuously numbered, as in the original score, though differences in how measures are counted cause Charpentier's total count of "821 mesures" (as he notes after the final barline) to be 755 in the edition.

The score of the edition begins with a full representation of the instrumental and vocal staves needed for the work but thereafter follows Charpentier's ordering of staves. Bracketed instrument and voice names have been added in the margin of the first system, followed by abbreviations for subsequent systems, using contemporary terms (dessus de violon, flûte, haute-contre de violon, taille de violon, basse continue for the instruments; dessus, haute-contre, taille, basse for the voices). Within the score Charpentier's original instrument and voice indications are retained, with brackets to mark the completion of his abbreviations (except for his "acc seul," which is spelled out only once and then is set as "acc. seul"); he generally placed these above the staves or in the margins for the upper parts, below the staff or in the margins for the basse continue part. In the edition the placements are regularized to appear above in the upper parts and below in the basse continue. Sectional headings in the work ("Praeludium," "Chorus Justorum," etc.) follow Charpentier, with some additional headings supplied in brackets. All of the part names and sectional headings have been regularized in the use of capitalized or lowercased letters.

In the edition, sectional double barlines have been added. Modern repeat barlines and first and second endings have been added as called for by the notation of the source. Beaming has generally been left as found in the source, except that in duple meter passages, beamed groups exceeding four notes have been broken to beam at the quarter note or half note, depending on the note values involved.

Charpentier's notation of accidentals includes a few conventions that differ from our modern ones, namely (1) the complete absence of naturals—only sharps and flats are used; (2) from time to time, Charpentier attaches a sharp (in the sense of a natural) to a note for which no such indication is necessary; and (3) accidentals are attached to every single note that is altered, without regard to barring. The present edition incorporates naturals in the parts and also in the continuo figures, and removes accidentals on tied notes over barlines, but otherwise reproduces all of Charpentier's conventions. Editorially added accidentals are placed in brackets.

Charpentier's key signatures likewise reflect pre-tonal norms. Thus, the opening "Praeludium" bears the signature of two flats even though the music is in what we would understand to be C minor. For this edition the original key signatures are not modernized, but instead are retained as they appear in the original.

The convention for indicating slurs differs from our modern practice as well. This poses few problems for the instrumental parts, but the use of slurring to indicate text underlay in the vocal parts produces certain unusual features. It works as follows: When beaming is present for eighth notes and the extent of the beaming coincides with the extent of a melisma, no slur is given, since text underlay is clear. When more than one group of beamed notes carries a single syllable of text, a slur is used to connect the last note of the first group to the first note of the second; these slurs have not been included in the edition. When no beaming is present, Charpentier uses individual slurs to connect at most three or four notes; in no case does a large slur cover a great many notes. Slurring is invariably clear in the manuscript and is rendered for the edition as described above; also, slurs are drawn to enclose ties in the edition. Only very rarely does the edition add a slur or tie in places where they are not present in the manuscript; all such are dashed. Individual cases of ambiguity are indicated in the critical notes.

Charpentier provides a great deal of figuring for the bass part, but his figures are by no means absolutely complete; editorially added figures have therefore been provided, appearing in brackets. On the other hand, Charpentier's text underlay is free of punctuation, and this has been added tacitly in the edition.

Critical Notes

Abbreviations referring to the edition are as follows: D = Dessus, HC = Haute-contre, T = Taille, B = Basse, D.vn. = Dessus de violon, Fl. = Flûte, Hc.vn. = Haute-contre de violon, T.vn. = Taille de violon, B.c. = Basse continue. Notes are numbered consecutively within a measure. Pitches are identified using the system in which c' = middle C.

In nativitatem Domini canticum

M. 33, T.vn., the indications appearing above and below the staff carry the feminine endings "P^{re}" and "S^{de}," but the masculine endings are used in mm. 485, 643, and 744; the edition follows the latter cases with reference to the general term "violon." M. 38, B.c., originally two tied half notes, notated this way because of a system break. M. 51, after this measure the source has the following note: "Suivez au choeur." M. 90, T.vn., note 4 was originally b♭', appears to be corrected to c" by copyist. Mm. 102–3, D, textual slurs connect m. 102, notes 1–2, and m. 103, notes 1–2; these are removed from the edition to leave only the source ties of mm. 101–3. Mm. 106–86, D.vn. 1 and Fl. 1, D.vn. 2 and Fl. 2, the source makes clear that both obbligato parts are played by dividing into two groups the players that have until this point played the top line; this is signaled not only by the cleffing (French violin clef for both parts) but by m. 186, the first note of which is stemmed both up and down (as shown in the edition); the indications "vio[lo]ns et fl[ûtes]" (for D.vn. 1 and Fl. 1) and "vio[lo]n[s] et fl[ûtes]" (for D.vn. 2 and Fl. 2) are given at m. 112 (system break) but presumably apply to the entire section beginning at m. 106. M. 155, B, note 2 is d, changed to c in edition to match B.c. part. Mm. 184–85, D.vn. 1 and Fl. 1, D.vn. 2 and Fl. 2, B1, B.c., source uses colored notation here, i.e., black noteheads without stems for whole notes and black notes with stems for half notes, to indicate the hemiola. M. 190, D.vn. 1-2 and Fl. 1-2, Charpentier originally wrote g" for note 1, which a later hand (Charpentier?) corrected to e♭" by simply adding a notehead; the latter matches the reading of HC, which the part doubles at this point, and must therefore be correct. Mm. 231–38, B, B.c., for these measures these two parts are notated as one ("orgue voix et vio[lo]ns" is written in the margin); m. 239 then continues with the B.c. part, leaving no final note for B; for this edition, B is given a whole note on the pitch of the first note in the B.c. part. M. 313, T.vn., in addition to the notes shown in the edition, the source has a semibreve g below them; this whole-note g appears to have been partially erased, but it is possible that the violas should divide for this measure. Mm. 321–22, after this two-measure rest the source has the following note: "Suivez apres les deux mesures de Silence," followed by page break. M. 323, top of next page: "Suite de la Nuit;" left margin: "sans fl[ûtes];" below D.vn. 1-2 and Hc.vn. parts: "sourd[ines]." M. 355, B.c., there seems to be an extraneous figure here, ⁵₅; the extra "5" is eliminated. M. 386, the indication "viste" appears below D.vn. 1-2 and Fl. 1-2, Hc.vn., T.vn., and B.c. staves; set as a score direction "Vite" in the edition. M. 433, Hc.vn., note 3 has ♯, changed to ♮ in edition for sake of harmony. M. 585, B.c., note 3 is d, changed to e in edition for harmony. Mm. 594–611, the repeat of this section is not indicated through repeat signs, but through the use of the word "reprise" written at m. 594 below the D.vn. 1-2 and Fl. 1-2 staff; set as a score direction in the edition. M. 652, HC, the indication above the staff refers to "l'Ange seule"; in the edition the masculine form is used with reference to "ange." M. 684, the indication "Ritor[nello]" appears below D.vn. 1-2 and Fl. 1-2, Hc.vn., T.vn., and B.c. staves; set as a score direction in the edition. M. 692, "tous" appears to left of HC staff; moved to m. 696 above B staff in edition.

Recent Researches in the Music of the Baroque Era
Christoph Wolff, general editor

Vol.	Composer: Title
1	Marc-Antoine Charpentier: *Judicium Salomonis*
2	Georg Philipp Telemann: *Forty-eight Chorale Preludes*
3	Johann Caspar Kerll: *Missa Superba*
4–5	Jean-Marie Leclair: *Sonatas for Violin and Basso continuo, Opus 5*
6	*Ten Eighteenth-Century Voluntaries*
7–8	William Boyce: *Two Anthems for the Georgian Court*
9	Giulio Caccini: *Le nuove musiche*
10–11	Jean-Marie Leclair: *Sonatas for Violin and Basso continuo, Opus 9 and Opus 15*
12	Johann Ernst Eberlin: *Te Deum; Dixit Dominus; Magnificat*
13	Gregor Aichinger: *Cantiones Ecclesiasticae*
14–15	Giovanni Legrenzi: *Cantatas and Canzonets for Solo Voice*
16	Giovanni Francesco Anerio and Francesco Soriano: *Two Settings of Palestrina's "Missa Papae Marcelli"*
17	Giovanni Paolo Colonna: *Messe a nove voci concertata con stromenti*
18	Michel Corrette: *"Premier livre d'orgue" and "Nouveau livre de noëls"*
19	Maurice Greene: *Voluntaries and Suites for Organ and Harpsichord*
20	Giovanni Antonio Piani: *Sonatas for Violin Solo and Violoncello with Cembalo*
21–22	Marin Marais: *Six Suites for Viol and Thoroughbass*
23–24	Dario Castello: *Selected Ensemble Sonatas*
25	*A Neapolitan Festa a Ballo and Selected Instrumental Ensemble Pieces*
26	Antonio Vivaldi: *The Manchester Violin Sonatas*
27	Louis-Nicolas Clérambault: *Two Cantatas for Soprano and Chamber Ensemble*
28	Giulio Caccini: *Nuove musiche e nuova maniera di scriverle (1614)*
29–30	Michel Pignolet de Montéclair: *Cantatas for One and Two Voices*
31	Tomaso Albinoni: *Twelve Cantatas, Opus 4*
32–33	Antonio Vivaldi: *Cantatas for Solo Voice*
34	Johann Kuhnau: *Magnificat*
35	Johann Stadlmayr: *Selected Magnificats*
36–37	Jacopo Peri: *Euridice: An Opera in One Act, Five Scenes*
38	Francesco Severi: *Salmi passaggiati (1615)*
39	George Frideric Handel: *Six Concertos for the Harpsichord or Organ (Walsh's Transcriptions, 1738)*
40	*The Brasov Tablature (Brasov Music Manuscript 808): German Keyboard Studies 1608–1684*
41	John Coprario: *Twelve Fantasias for Two Bass Viols and Organ and Eleven Pieces for Three Lyra Viols*

42	Antonio Cesti: *Il pomo d'oro (Music for Acts III and V from Modena, Biblioteca Estense, Ms. Mus. E. 120)*
43	Tomaso Albinoni: *Pimpinone: Intermezzi comici musicali*
44–45	Antonio Lotti: *Duetti, terzetti, e madrigali a piu voci*
46	Matthias Weckmann: *Four Sacred Concertos*
47	Jean Gilles: *Requiem (Messe des morts)*
48	Marc-Antoine Charpentier: *Vocal Chamber Music*
49	*Spanish Art Song in the Seventeenth Century*
50	Jacopo Peri: *"Le varie musiche" and Other Songs*
51–52	Tomaso Albinoni: *Sonatas and Suites, Opus 8, for Two Violins, Violoncello, and Basso continuo*
53	Agostino Steffani: *Twelve Chamber Duets*
54–55	Gregor Aichinger: *The Vocal Concertos*
56	Giovanni Battista Draghi: *Harpsichord Music*
57	*Concerted Sacred Music of the Bologna School*
58	Jean-Marie Leclair: *Sonatas for Violin and Basso continuo, Opus 2*
59	Isabella Leonarda: *Selected Compositions*
60–61	Johann Schelle: *Six Chorale Cantatas*
62	Denis Gaultier: *La Rhétorique des Dieux*
63	Marc-Antoine Charpentier: *Music for Molière's Comedies*
64–65	Georg Philipp Telemann: *Don Quichotte auf der Hochzeit des Comacho: Comic Opera-Serenata in One Act*
66	Henry Butler: *Collected Works*
67–68	John Jenkins: *The Lyra Viol Consorts*
69	*Keyboard Transcriptions from the Bach Circle*
70	Melchior Franck: *Geistliche Gesäng und Melodeyen*
71	Georg Philipp Telemann: *Douze solos, à violon ou traversière*
72	Marc-Antoine Charpentier: *Nine Settings of the "Litanies de la Vierge"*
73	*The Motets of Jacob Praetorius II*
74	Giovanni Porta: *Selected Sacred Music from the Ospedale della Pietà*
75	*Fourteen Motets from the Court of Ferdinand II of Hapsburg*
76	Jean-Marie Leclair: *Sonatas for Violin and Basso continuo, Opus 1*
77	Antonio Bononcini: *Complete Sonatas for Violoncello and Basso continuo*
78	Christoph Graupner: *Concerti Grossi for Two Violins*
79	Paolo Quagliati: *Il primo libro de' madrigali a quattro voci*
80	Melchior Franck: *Dulces Mundani Exilij Deliciae*
81	*Late-Seventeenth-Century English Keyboard Music*
82	*Solo Compositions for Violin and Viola da gamba with Basso continuo*
83	Barbara Strozzi: *Cantate, ariete a una, due e tre voci, Opus 3*
84	Charles-Hubert Gervais: *Super flumina Babilonis*

85	Henry Aldrich: *Selected Anthems and Motet Recompositions*
86	Lodovico Grossi da Viadana: *Salmi a quattro cori*
87	Chiara Margarita Cozzolani: *Motets*
88	Elisabeth-Claude Jacquet de La Guerre: *Cephale et Procris*
89	Sébastien Le Camus: *Airs à deux et trois parties*
90	Thomas Ford: *Lyra Viol Duets*
91	*Dedication Service for St. Gertrude's Chapel, Hamburg, 1607*
92	Johann Klemm: *Partitura seu Tabulatura italica*
93	Giovanni Battista Somis: *Sonatas for Violin and Basso continuo, Opus 3*
94	John Weldon: *The Judgment of Paris*
95–96	Juan Bautista Comes: *Masses. Parts 1–2*
97	Sebastian Knüpfer: *Lustige Madrigalien und Canzonetten*
98	Stefano Landi: *La morte d'Orfeo*
99	Giovanni Battista Fontana: *Sonatas for One, Two, and Three Parts with Basso continuo*
100	Georg Philipp Telemann: *Twelve Trios*
101	Fortunato Chelleri: *Keyboard Music*
102	Johann David Heinichen: *La gara degli Dei*
103	Johann David Heinichen: *Diana su l'Elba*
104	Alessandro Scarlatti: *Venere, Amore e Ragione*
105	*Songs with Theorbo (ca. 1650–1663)*
106	Melchior Franck: *Paradisus Musicus*
107	Heinrich Ignaz Franz von Biber: *Missa Christi resurgentis*
108	Johann Ludwig Bach: *Motets*
109–10	Giovanni Rovetta: *Messa, e salmi concertati, op. 4 (1639). Parts 1–2*
111	Johann Joachim Quantz: *Seven Trio Sonatas*
112	Petits motets *from the Royal Convent School at Saint Cyr*
113	Isabella Leonarda: *Twelve Sonatas, Opus 16*
114	Rudolph di Lasso: *Virginalia Eucharistica (1615)*
115	Giuseppe Torelli: *Concerti musicali, Opus 6*
116–17	Nicola Francesco Haym: *Complete Sonatas. Parts 1–2*
118	Benedetto Marcello: *Il pianto e il riso delle quattro stagioni*
119	Loreto Vittori: *La Galatea*
120–23	William Lawes: *Collected Vocal Music. Parts 1–4*
124	Marco da Gagliano: *Madrigals. Part 1*
125	Johann Schop: *Erster Theil newer Paduanen*
126	Giovanni Felice Sances: *Motetti a una, due, tre, e quattro voci (1638)*
127	Thomas Elsbeth: *Sontägliche Evangelien*
128–30	Giovanni Antonio Rigatti: *Messa e salmi, parte concertati. Parts 1–3*

131	*Seventeenth-Century Lutheran Church Music with Trombones*
132	Francesco Cavalli: *La Doriclea*
133	*Music for "Macbeth"*
134	Domenico Allegri: *Music for an Academic Defense (Rome, 1617)*
135	Jean Gilles: *Diligam te, Domine*
136	Silvius Leopold Weiss: *Lute Concerti*
137	*Masses by Alessandro Scarlatti and Francesco Gasparini*
138	Giovanni Ghizzolo: *Madrigali et arie per sonare et cantare*
139	Michel Lambert: *Airs from "Airs de différents autheurs"*
140	William Babell: *Twelve Solos for a Violin or Oboe with Basso Continuo. Book 1*
141	Giovanni Francesco Anerio: *Selva armonica (Rome, 1617)*
142–43	Bellerofonte Castaldi: *Capricci (1622). Parts 1–2*
144	Georg von Bertouch: *Sonatas a 3*
145	Marco da Gagliano: *Madrigals. Part 2*
146	Giovanni Rovetta: *Masses*
147	Giacomo Antonio Perti: *Five-Voice Motets for the Assumption of the Virgin Mary*
148	Giovanni Felice Sances: *Motetti a 2, 3, 4, e cinque voci (1642)*
149	*La grand-mére amoureuse, parodie d'Atys*
150	Andreas Hammerschmidt: *Geistlicher Dialogen Ander Theil*
151	Georg von Bertouch: *Three Sacred Cantatas*
152	Giovanni Maria Ruggieri: *Two Settings of the Gloria*
153	Alessandro Scarlatti: *Concerti sacri, opera seconda*
154	Johann Sigismund Kusser: *Adonis*
155	John Blow: *Selected Verse Anthems*
156	Anton Holzner: *Viretum pierium (1621)*
157	Alessandro Scarlatti: *Venere, Adone, et Amore*
158	Marc-Antoine Charpentier: *In nativitatem Domini canticum, H. 416*